Praise for Judas &

"Rarely, if ever, have I read such an honest and artistic exploration of what it means to have to develop a will to live. Williams writes about suicide and suicidal ideation with a vulnerability and complexity that is only possible through lived experience. This book is one small, but crucial, step toward destigmatizing suicide in society and one large leap in helping those who have had their lives touched by it feel less alone."

—Allison Raskin, Author of *Overthinking About You: Navigating Romantic Relationships When You Have Anxiety, OCD, and/or Depression*

"How about we try living? Maya Williams writes in the persona of Paul the Apostle, and this book shows me how to try to live—this book is that good good prayer, it is a gust of wind that lifts my feet from beneath me. Across the poetry collection, Williams uses certain poetic forms (for example: the ghazal, the villanelle, and the sestina) to express the entrapment of trauma, the cycle of depression, and the tension within the speaker to break out of its forms. Williams is impeccable at curating fragmented images and voices to create a landscape in which the speaker navigates the living, the past, and the despair found in religion. Like summer rains being the occasional cleanse we desire with its liveliness within the gray, this book is the summer rain that reminds me that I am alive, that I am here to stay, and that I am grateful that Maya Williams, and their poems, are here to stay as well."

—Joshua Nguyen, Author of *Come Clean*

"In this powerful and necessary collection, Maya helps us navigate what it means to struggle, commit to, and celebrate survival. Maya shows us it's okay to have 'grief for past versions of yourself' in poems that unapologetically interrogate prayer, frustration, communication, and human connection."

—Tanaya Winder, Author of *Words Like Love*

"Maya Williams will change the way you see the world. I couldn't shake these stunning poems, and I'm sure I never will. I want to put this vital collection in the hands of everyone I know."

—Chris Stedman, Author of *IRL* and Creator, Writer, and Host of *Unread*

"Where was Maya Williams when I was a suicidal teen? The answer, of course, is living the experiences that allowed them to write with the kind of radical authenticity and fearlessness that can only come from someone who has seen, felt, and reveled in, all of the vividest depths and edges of human emotion. This is a revolution in book form. Every poem within honors survival as not only a choice, but (for those of us who have been driven to test an *Alternative Future*), a choice we must make again and again. Maya's poems fill me with hope for the readers who have yet to feel their empathy resonate from the pages, and by it feel that much more empowered in the decision to stay."

—Katya Zinn, Author of *Manic-depressive Pixie Dream Girl* and *human verses*

"*Judas & Suicide* is filled with crucial work for the church baby, for the Black child and for you. Williams writes about suicidal ideation honestly and the shadow religious trauma casts while simultaneously orchestrating the link between Bible stories and mental health. This is an essential collection that knocks the reader off their feet, embraces them and invites you to survive."

—Raych Jackson, Author of *Even the Saints Audition*

"I am learning how to only pray in an honest state / of mind," writes Maya Williams near the midpoint of *Judas & Suicide*—and their work is a radiant, righteous and restorative guidestar for such a journey. This debut resonates with the boldness and clarity of bell hooks, who challenges us to believe: 'There can be no love without justice.' With great ferocity and grace, Williams takes on that faith through these poems. They reckon with the grievances we bear while also illuminating 'an alternate universe of light that exists out there' and within all of us."

—R.A. Villanueva, Author of *Reliquaria*

"There are four poems titled *If You Stop Crying, It Won't Hurt As Much* in Maya Williams poetry collection *Judas & Suicide*. In titles such as this, the reader is brought into the tension that is at the heart of so much of this extraordinary collection of poetry: the tension between a title and a line; the tension between wanting help but rejecting unhelpful help; the tension between not wanting to die and wanting to live. In dexterous form, through multiple voices, registers and allusions, Maya Williams asserts a vibrant poetry that has, at its core, understood itself, and asks to be understood."

—Pádraig Ó Tuama, Host of Poetry *Unbound* from *On Being Studios*, Author of *Poetry Unbound; Fifty Poems to Open Your World and Feed the Beast.*

"A masterful and thought-provoking examination of where mental health meets religion, *Judas & Suicide* gives a voice to the far too long, silenced. This collection leads its readers to confront what it means to grapple with the question of living, in an environment that often invalidates the strength it takes to choose life. Williams bravely ushers us through these difficult truths with compassion, nuance, and keen understanding. Refreshingly humanizing, *Judas & Suicide* offers hope in place of solution, and makes space for 'the sinner' to be seen."

—Lindsay Young, Author of *Salt to Taste* and *In Your Absence*

" 'Mental illness unravels like a motherfucker,' writes Maya Williams in their debut poetry collection, *Judas & Suicide*. Throughout this book, Williams skillfully traverses complicated topics with clear images and straightforward language. If I wrote down every line that I loved, this blurb would be its own book."

—Paige Lewis, Author of *Space Struck*

"Maya writes in courageous, spirallic time, anticipating a world where poetry is the foundation of wellness curriculums in schools across the country. This is the work of the artist, not just to model vulnerability but to guide us internally and socially."

—Indira Allegra, United States Artists Fellow

"I thought I was ready to have a text undo my sense of self when I first encountered the poetry of June Jordan and Claudia Rankine. Somehow these two voices unraveled me in ways that can only be described as prayer and witness: they ushered me into my own complexity, sitting me at the altar of my own body, and then wrapping me in the divine presence of words. Maya Williams in *Judas & Suicide* does just that. She is a part of a long tradition that somehow finds a way to mix prose and politics, mourning and joy, wrestling and resting, vulnerability and celebration, reminding the reading the pain is not all we hold. We also hold treasure and creativity and life. This text bleeds with love, weaving the horrifying and humorous parts of our lives into one beautiful experience. This book is like that like that like that."

—Danté Stewart, Author of *Shoutin' in the Fire: an American Epistle*

Judas & Suicide

Poems by

Maya Williams

Judas & Suicide

ISBN: 979-8-9878871-0-3

Cover design and layout by Catherine Weiss.

Edited by Sara Mae and Josh Savory.

GAME OVER BOOKS

www.gameoverbooks.com

Curse

Commit

Watch

Forgive

Stay

Alive

for Michael, Jon, Sylvie, Tom, and more

"I've had a long life of wanting to not be alive."

—*Ideation* by Sam Sax

"Just 'cause your life falls apart doesn't mean you have to lose your desire to live it."

—*What to do when your life falls apart* by Anna Akana

In *the* Beginning

God was bored, lonely, and loving enough to allow himself to pull the glittery Big Bang from His sleeve. Lucifer was bored too, but while not too far from God, he liked the loneliness of the darkness.

God said, *Let there be light* when He created the day, and proclaimed it good. Lucifer thought his name provided enough light.

On the day God created Adam, Lucifer questioned his own enoughness. When God did not want man to be alone, and made a companion for Adam, Lucifer became jealous. Bitter.

When Adam and Eve were kicked out of Eden, Lucifer did not expect to be cursed too. To be alone, and God having more than enough friends.

I'll show Him, thought Lucifer.

On the twelfth day, Lucifer changed his name to Satan, and proclaimed it good.

On the one thousand and ninety-sixth day, Satan challenged God to show how hopeless humans are through Job. Prove to Him that slinging out creation was never a good idea. God, righteously cocky, said, *Bet.*

God won, and it was good.

Satan rubbed his hands together and got to work. *Try again.*

On the two hundred and sixty thousand six hundred and sixty-sixth day, Satan created white supremacy, the DSM, transphobia. Continued to trick scattered humans into believing any room for sorrow becomes a room for damnation. Sitting back on his recliner engulfed by flames, he enjoyed witnessing humans shout at God from afar.

Satan's favorite saying humans created for him is *The greatest trick The Devil ever pulled was making the world believe he didn't exist.*

On the trillionth day, Satan continues to destroy and confuse humans to get that original loneliness back, and he finds it oh so good.

Curse

Side Effects of Prayer

after Shira Erlichman

Side effects to prayer may include (enlightenment, a closer relationship to God, questioning who the fuck God thinks He is, scratching due to lack of other grounding techniques, frustration, reading scripture, a forced linear relationship with God, questioning all the people and systems who told us our relationship with God had to be linear, answered/unanswered/half answered/incorrectly answered prayers, the ability to crave signs, the ability to assign free will or fate, performative survival, survival that gradually feels more real, seeking multiple definitions of the word *miracle*, therapy despite your family members' protests, isolation that helps, isolation that doesn't, community that helps, community that doesn't, trying to bless or damn something yourself, writing prayers to have personal receipts of how much God has accomplished, writing prayers to have personal receipts of how much bad shit God allowed to happen, seeking multiple definitions of the word *evil*, making Christians upset for finding humor in nonreligious jokes, making Christians upset) having grief for past versions of yourself.

Jonah, Suicide, & *GOD Doesn't Give You ANY More Than YOU CAN HANDLE*

after Raych Jackson

"So now, Lord, kill me instead, because I would rather die than live!"
—Jonah 4:3 NET

GOD has given JONAH a LOT that HE COULDN'T HANDLE.

That's WHY when he had to GO to NINEVEH, he tried his BEST to AVOID IT.

GOD has given ME a LOT that I COULDN'T HANDLE.

That's WHY when I had to GO to THERAPY, I tried my BEST to AVOID IT.

GOD has given JONAH a LOT HE COULDN'T HANDLE.

That's WHY he THOUGHT to END his LIFE before the GREAT FISH COULD.

GOD has given ME a LOT I COULDN'T HANDLE.

That's WHY I THOUGHT to END my LIFE before the GREAT FISH CALLED "LIFE" COULD.

GOD has given JONAH a LOT HE COULDN'T HANDLE.

That's WHY when the PEOPLE OF NINEVEH wouldn't LISTEN he questioned why he DIDN'T AVOID THEM.

GOD has given ME a LOT I COULDN'T HANDLE.

That's WHY when the PEOPLE OF MY FAMILY wouldn't LISTEN

I questioned why I DIDN'T AVOID THEM.

GOD has given JONAH a LOT HE COULDN'T HANDLE.

That's WHY he THOUGHT of ENDING HIS LIFE AGAIN after the GREAT FISH COULDN'T.

GOD has GIVEN me A LOT that I COULDN'T handle.

That's WHY I THOUGHT of ENDING MY LIFE AGAIN after the GREAT FISH CALLED "LIFE" COULDN'T.

GOD allowed OUR FISH to SWALLOW us WHOLE.

If You Stop Crying, It Won't Hurt As Much

It is another Saturday night when "Pour Me a Shot of Whisky" plays on my grandmother's stereo as she, my mother, my aunt, my uncle, and my play cousins are drinking in the dining room. Eight year old me runs to the dining room crying from another headache. My aunt rushes me to the shower and runs out for Advil to help me feel better.

My aunt is the first to teach me that the more I cried, the more it would hurt.

Curses, Suicide, & *Just Pray About It*

So the unclean spirits came out and went into the pigs. Then the herd rushed down the steep slope into the lake, and about two thousand were drowned in the lake.

—Mark 5:13 NET

I jump off and hold my breath.

There on the hillside, a great herd of pigs was feeding.

My father
asks
Can you focus

And the demonic spirits begged him,

on having fun
today
at the lake house?

There is
trouble
in your spirit

'Send us into the pigs. Let us enter them.'

Bubbles rev through my nose as I sink.

My father
says
you can't change the past.

Jesus gave them permission.

He never
says
that

when I describe a
positive
memory to him.

So the unclean spirits came out and went into the pigs.

I want to keep myself from floating up.

I try to I hold it all
in
so the lake can swallow me.

Then the herd rushed down the steep slope into the lake,

The coward
in me
returns for air.

My dad
affirms
curses can be broken.

Just
pray
about
it.

I did not conjure my depression.

I do not
tell
him

there is little to no
correlation
between prayer and wellness.

I ask if we can go
swimming
again tomorrow afternoon.

and about two thousand were drowned in the lake.

Google Search History, Age 15

How do I spell masterbate?
Does masturbating cause STDs?
Does masturbating count as sex?
Does masturbating to girls make me like girls?
What does the Bible say about masturbating?
How long does it take to fall in love?
When is the best time to say I love you?
What is love?
Who can love me?
How do I know I'm depressed?
How do I know I need medication?
How do I not kill myself?
What is another word for killing yourself?
How many people have killed themselves?
What does the Bible say about killing yourself?

A Facebook Message from My Stepmother

your father
never shared

once tried to discuss
suicidal thoughts dad

cut me off told me

I'm stronger
than this
never tried
to self medicate

don't think of
suicide anymore

                                Pray
for your dad

he will   struggle
with   demons. He prays but
could continue   forever with
this
                            your heart
            judges
      loss

Before Taking Prozac for the First Time

The headaches will feel
like a watermelon
being split

Haven't you had
many slices
before this?

4-6
weeks is a long time
to wait
for a change

10-15
years was much
longer
than that

My
phone call
with Dad
wasn't great

At least
your calls
with Mom and stepmom
were better

I'll have to grieve
the way
my brain
used to be

Whether it's fluoxetine
or another med later
maybe you won't have
to grieve at all.

Sick Boy

America

lies

and expects you to listen to 'em
prison
is
sick

America

lies

and expects you to listen to ‘em
prison
is
sick

Feed s
 o n   life
Feed s
 o n   life
Feed s
 o n   life
Feed s
 o n   life

Commit

When a Falmouth Police Officer Pulls You Over to Call Your Panic Attack Drunkenness

Cry

Pray

Sob

Wail

Repeat

Pull over
when his red, blue, and white lights flicker.

Show him your ID
Your skin may be lighter than
your brother's, but your hair is still kinky.
You can only assume that's why the
flashlight's work shift begins.

Thank God
you are wearing a blue blouse
that covers your cleavage and
your pulse rattling back and forth
in your chest.

Assert calmly
that you are, indeed, one of the good ones,
not drunk. It's just a late night.

Thank God
you updated your flimsy
registration and insurance slips in time.

Don't remember to breathe
You're sure he and his American flag colored lights
don't want you to. Use that PWI college education
of yours to push that politeness as if you are pedal pushing
the gas to leave.

Push down the panic crawling up
from your chest to your esophagus
to your mouth earlier on the road.
Don't tell either of them
about your mental disorder.
They'll use it against you.

When the officer
tells you *Just wanted to check in*. Lie
to him and the flashlight intimidating your
eyes and say you believe them both.
That you believe their goodcopbadcop
routine.

Cry

Pray

Sob

Wail

Repeat

Give in
to your fear of the officer
and his lights following you
home. Or pulling you over

again. Or pulling over someone
else. Or arresting someone else.
Or arresting you.

Question
if you can breathe.

Thank them.
Wish them a good night.
Drive 10 miles under the speed limit
assigned to you
and fellow drivers.

I Hate to Go Inside a Building Created to Destroy Me

At least I get to leave it.
At least I get to return home.
Not a guarantee I'll get home safely,
but it's a possibility.

I hate the gray device with the red button they give us
upon entry. We are supposed to press it
if any *residents* give us trouble.
We have never needed the extra weight.

I hate that a white C.O. can show up on
Bumble in his uniform.
I throw my phone across the room
when I see that for the first time.

I hate when a Black C.O. gives me eye contact
to expect solidarity from me.
I cannot
give it.

I hate that I have been mistaken
as a *resident.*
How often staff have desired
to say to my face *welcome home.*

In Defense of Commit in Relation to Suicide on Trial

Exhibits A-F

It is a "commitment" to accountability.
It is a "commitment" to follow through.
It is a "condemnation" of one's own life.
It is a "condemnation" of the burden of breath.
It is a "call" to what those left behind do not want.
It is a "call" to an action those left behind cannot stop in time.

Verdict:

The plaintiff doesn't know the difference between criminalizing the act and criminalizing the person. To hate the sin and love the sinner.

Two Weeks After Taking Prozac for the First Time

What is
the difference
between
the reality
of the pills
and the reality
of my life?

Who is
to say
they aren't
one
in the same?

My anxiety
has been a spark
for so long.
I'm not productive
as before.

Praise
the day
you finally
ceased
to be a machine.

It was so hard
to wake up
a few
days
ago.

But
it was
easier
today,

wasn't it?

Analysis of Tension in *Depressed*

"-ed" refers to the past

It's not in the past.

Watch

If You Stop Crying, It Won't Hurt As Much

It is summer vacation and it is time to move boxes out of our blue house in Charlotte and into a white Uhaul for a red brick house in Greensboro. Fifteen year old me feels the sweat and heavy breath hold my body captive. I continue to rush as I liftwalkdroprepeat with as much helpful precision as I can despite the tears constantly dripping down my face.

My stepdad and my mother laugh at me. They tell me that if I try to stop crying, my body wouldn't hurt as much.

Extension

Fourteen year old me was always ready to rumble and tumble
with the question of the right femininity to fit
cis girlhood.[1]
Sixteen year old me was always ready to rumble and tumble
with the question of my mother and sisters' frustration with
my baggier clothes.[2]
Nineteen year old me was always ready to rumble and tumble
with the question of why I got a pixie cut that everyone
except my brother hated.[3]

---

1 Most cartoon animators enforce the gender binary by creating eyelashes for girls, while there are no eyelashes for boys. On one end, it's nice to extend femininity visually. On another, why not let masculinity extend itself? An overused statement online for a while was, *A guy should mess up your lipstick, not your mascara.* ...But my mascara is waterproof. There's a lack of trust there, and the lack of eyelashes for cis men only increases my distrust. My mascara, my lipstick, stays firmly, properly, on.

2 When I point out evidence of my mother and my sisters' negative feedback about my clothes that *did* fit and feminize, they said, *At least you were trying harder then.* I was raised to please their gaze. I was socialized to please men's gaze. Although cis women in my family thought I was trying to see if boyhood could fit on me, I was trying to navigate what being genderless meant. Did genderless mean I didn't have to try? If the women in my family knew I was faking by how hard I was trying, why did they criticize instead of help me?

3 It must have been hard for my brother growing up around so many women. It must have been hard for my brother to find the right extension of masculinity for himself. It must have been hard for him to trust me enough to talk about it. I certainly didn't trust him.

Judas Does Not Deserve My Sympathy

Andrew,
if you think I am going to sympathize with Judas
because he's consistently cast as Black,
think again.

You come from a long line of musical creators
who used marginalized identity
to fetishize and produce audience tears
to praise you all for
nuance.

First, there was George.
Later, he begat Oscar.
Who later begat Richard.
Who later begat Leonard.
Who later begat *you.*

They weren't shit, you ain't shit,
and neither is Judas.

Maybe you want us to sympathize with him
because he's a reflection of you.
A minstrel emotional provocateur
of your making.

Maybe you want us to sympathize with him
so you can be as savior-adjacent
as you thought the white men
you cast as Jesus were.

Maybe you want us to sympathize with him
because God don't make
mistakes,
humans do.

You and Judas ain't The Devil,
but y'all ain't God either.

What Are You Two Watching?

Irritated see

loudly she's crying

watching for the tenth time

Dead Poets Society

suicide dramatic

because whisper

I'm trapped

It Hurts a Lot More When the Reports are Right

I attempted suicide when I was fifteen.

Suicide rates rise in a generation of Black youth feels like a punch in the gut.

Higher prevalence of sexual assault amongst transgender and nonbinary adolescents feels like a kick in the cunt.

LGBTQ+ rates of suicide, especially amongst youth, are disproportionately higher than cisgender heterosexual individuals feels like a personal attack.

But, when I read that Black people's suicide rate is *still lower than the overall population's* because of *faith-based outreach*, I wonder

how many of us are pressured into leaving our questions unanswered?
how many of us are pressured into leaving our healing underwhelmed?
how many of us are pressured into staying alive quietly?
how many of us are pressured into staying alive than not?

When Someone You Know Dies by Suicide Again

after Camonghne Felix

You recognize how it hurts to admit how often Suicide has a point.
If Suicide is a solution to a temporary problem, why must the problem
become permanent as punishment for continuing to live?
A youth attempts to sign Suicide's offer with a bedsheet as the paper
and the gasps from his windpipe the ink,
a C.O. coos, *Do it.*
A trans woman drives home from a peer support group,
exhaling exhaustive signatures,
you will never know the full complexity of the forces that convince her,
Do it.
The same week an adult chooses to stay
tearing his contract to shreds,
a different adult chooses to leave.
What made one *Do it* stronger than the other? Survivor's Guilt
is a stone thrown at your sternum
each time you live longer than your loved ones.
You wish the stone would hurt you enough
to want to join your loved ones, and you feel even worse
that all the stones can do is hurt.
You aren't in the same headspace as your loved ones were
right now. Yes, that is a good thing; and it isn't
enough to numb the bruises or the breaking of your bones. No,
this does not discount the loved ones who still choose to live
alongside you. You swear you are grateful
for their bandages.

You remind yourself that there are more people
alive now
than anyone in the past who has died.

You remind yourself
of how there are humans
doing better
at convincing us
to stick around.

Forgive

Google Search History, Age 25

Children's songs and racism
"Working on the railroad" racist
"I've been working on the railroad" full lyrics
"Someone's in the kitchen with Dinah"
Black women slaves and Dinah
Slavery and women in the Bible
Rape in the Bible
Dinah in the Bible
Dinah "defiled"
Dinah raped

If You Stop Crying, It Won't Hurt As Much

It is early fall and nineteen year old me and my boyfriend sit on my long, thin dorm bed. My poster of a rainbow painted bird has better eye contact with him than I do.

My boyfriend tells me to stop being manipulative with my tears. I try to stop crying so his words won't hurt as much.

Greenville, North Carolina 2017

he said he didn't
hear me
scream

his fingers
lacked
tenderness

after, my vagina
did
too

his arms
contained less
comfort than my tears

he said he didn't
mean
to
hurt
me

you two
shouldn't have slept
in the same bed

you
shouldn't have cheated
on him

you shouldn't have tried
to break
up with him

you shouldn't
have invited
him over

Have I Forgiven You?

My capacity to forgive you fluctuates.
There are days I don't even think about you,
though the strongest memory of harm recapitulates.

Now when my mind is triggered, my body no longer frustrates.
At least not all the time, I can't completely erase you.
My capacity to efface you fluctuates.

It is a calmer day when I can feel great.
When I feel I can honestly pray for you.
Though it's still hard when the strongest memory of harm recapitulates.

I am learning how to only pray in a honest state
of mind. It gives me comfort to not know how you
are doing or living as life non-linearly fluctuates.

I am still reconditioning how memory invalidates
me while making sure to validate you.
It surprises me when legitimately kind memories of you recapitulate.

Living a life without you is one I don't believe complicates
my need for affirmation; and I believe I will slowly forgive you.
My capacity to forgive you fluctuates
because of all the echoes of you that recapitulate.

The Last Day I Saw My Ex

I remember the teal floral dress I wore because of the pictures my sister took.

I don't remember if he wore glasses in front of his squinted eyes or not.

I remember why I invited him after our break up.

I don't remember what exactly made him come.

I remember asking him to take a picture of me with my professor.

I don't remember how many he took before demanding to speak to me.

I remember my neck and shoulders becoming stiff.

I don't remember all his pouted lips muttered to me.

I remember him spitting out *Fuck you.*

I don't remember when my sister stomped over to us, but she told me she saw his arm blocking my way to her.

I remember him scolding, *Do you even know what she did?*

I don't remember if he pointed at me while doing so.

I remember my cheating before the breakup.

I wonder if he remembers his gaslighting or manipulation.

I remember my sister’s deep furrowed eyebrows when she shouted, *Leave or I’ll call the cops!*

I don’t remember when he walked away.

I remember the tension leaving my shoulders, but not my neck.

I don’t remember if my sister or my peers asked if I was okay.

I remember my sister advising I don’t reach out to him again.

I don’t remember the time he called me to cry and apologize.

I remember posing next to the purple pirate mascot, smiling for my sister to take the remaining photos.

I don’t remember if we went to eat or went to my dorm room straight after.

I remember it being a nice day out.

I don’t remember if it stayed that way.

Stay

Samson & Suicide

Samson said, 'Let me die with the Philistines!' He pushed hard, and the temple collapsed on the rulers and all the people in it. He killed many more people in his death than he had killed during his life.
—Judges 16:30 NET

From the moment Samson
had his hair cut
he let go
of his strength
his sheets
his lion carcass trophy
his indulgence in honey
his riddles
his ex's tears
his kingdom
his team of fellow soldiers
his parents' respect
his ropes
his shackles

He took people
with him and was praised for it.

I thought
that cutting my hair
would help me let go.

I refused to take anyone
with me.

When Your White Partner Offers to Drive You Through Falmouth Next Time

Let him.

Convince Us to Stay

What most people don't understand about suicidal ideation
is how hella convinced we have to be to stay on this Earth.
Some days, even, *want* to stay. It's not enough to tell us
we'll burden someone if we leave, as often as we think
we'll burden someone if we stay. Ideation is the double-edged sword
we never asked for. Then again, we never asked to be *alive* either.
Ideation is the pendulum that swings from one alternate universe of darkness
to another. Convince us of an alternate universe of light that exists out there.
With less clichés this time. With more clichés we can be proud of.
With natural prayers. With no empty prayers at all.
Convince us of a better future ahead
without the pressure of having to fucking think of one.
Convince us of possibilities
without providing us *fucking barriers* in the same breath.
Hear us. Commend us
for our survival without us having to experience the threat
of a disappearance in the first place. *Need us*. No, I mean,
really, need us. Not because it'll make *you* feel better.
Because it'll make *all of us* feel better. No, I mean,
really, feel better. Like freedom of life
without giving compensation for saving it
after failed attempts. Like summer rains
being the occasional cleanse we desire
with its liveliness
within the gray. Like being
so fucking present
being
a blessed gift in of itself;
only no one has to wrap or re-wrap it for us.
Mental illness unravels
like a motherfucker. Convince us of the belief
that we can wrap and re-wrap it ourselves.

When Having Suicidal Thoughts Again

Remind yourself of how much it hurt when loved ones
attempted to be dead.

Remind yourself of how much it hurt when loved ones
became dead.

Remind yourself of how when your best friend attempted, you told them
you *want* to run out of poems for the dead.

Remind yourself of how you told them you *will not*
write a poem for *them* if they are dead.

Remind yourself, Maya, of how your best friend *will not*
write a poem for *you* if you are dead.

The Devil is Concerned with More Pressing Matters Than My Mental Health Issues

I won't deny.
He sure has been the ghost writer of most of the DSM.
Transforming transness into evil corrupt contagion.
Softening the blow of racism by labeling it
aimless.

I won't lie.
A theologian once described Jesus as his favorite ex-boyfriend who checks in.
I thought my least favorite was The Devil
with his unwelcome arrival in spirit.

But he is way too busy to be the spirit that possesses me.

The Devil has an apocalypse to plan.
Filled with red-orange flames from the arrows of trusty horsemen.
A supremacist army with desire for hell's manifest destiny.
Eugenic colonial power.

He has other curses to conjure
that have zero correlation with mental illness.
Emotions do not equate an ailment.
There is a difference between the thoughts I can control
and the thoughts I cannot.

Yes, pray for me. Only, pray the right one next time.

Good Good Prayer

I want that good good prayer

Not that *Talk to GOD so you don't have to talk to me* prayer

I want that *Talk to GOD so you can talk to your people how you need to* prayer

I want that good good prayer

Not that *Welcome the LORD into your heart pontificating in public* prayer

I want that *Welcome the LORD into your heart privately when you're ready* prayer

I want that good good prayer

Not that *Sending thoughts and prayers* prayer
from aimless Facebook comments
or check in text messages
impulsively obligatory
while full of permission to forget

I want that *I'm making my prayers float and move*
beyond my bedroom prayer
that lead to holding someone
or advocating in a way
impulsively obligatory
while full of permission to remember

I want that good good prayer

Not that *GOD doesn't want you swearing or speaking in slang* prayer

I want that juicy
colorful
honest prayer

I want that good good prayer

Not that *he's in a better place* prayer
I want that *he was taken against his will so how do we give others better reasons to stick around* prayer

I want that good good prayer

Not that *GOD is not calling us to that now* surface level prayer

I want that *GOD is calling to us and we're not leaving the sanctuary until we're done* prayer

Contracts

My therapist once told me,

You don't s t r i k e me

as someone who

fears

Death.

I

blame

knowing

Death

pretty well.

We're not friends,

but we're not foes either.

Our relationship

is purely transactional.

Death promised me wondrous gifts

Life couldn't offer:

Heaven, Quiet, The End

of Pain.

My suicide notes

were Death putting

the promises in writing.

Life may have stepped in

time

for me

to s h r e d t h e c o n t r a c t s

but

Death

still

kept

the offer in cold storage.

Even when Life was treating me better,

Death still seemed appealing.

Ideation was f i l l e d with Death's gifts.

I didn't intend to unwrap them.

Death

still checks in on me

when an episode

strikes

me,

when Life

fails

another

loved one.

Still

it's nice to know

I'm not afraid

of Death

for a completely different reason now.

Our negotiation will come naturally;

not forced through suicide notes.

Judas & Suicide

So Judas threw the silver coins into the temple and left. Then he went out and hanged himself.
—Matthew 27: 3-5 NET

My grandmother thought
women with mental illnesses in our family
were like Judas.

Judas.
Cowardly.
Betrayer of the disciples; Betrayer of Jesus.

Hanged himself not for being sorry,
but to escape blame.
Jesus died *for* our sins while Judas died *by* his.

Despite clear scripture of Judas' death
there are blurred lines in between where
his death is viewed as a sin, like his duplicity.

He killed Jesus
and himself.
Thou shalt not kill, right?

My cousin has bipolar disorder.
After her attempt,
my grandmother thought she was

Cowardly.
Betrayer of the family.
Betrayer of my grandmother.

Took
pills
as a way out.

I have obsessive compulsive disorder.
I mention my attempt,
my grandmother says I'm not like my cousin.

A problem child.
Always going through something;
craving her big escape.

I have it together.
Always keeping busy;
I stay away from making mistakes.

I ask,
Are you
sure?

My grandmother
doesn't
understand.

She thought things were going well for me.
Why would I want to hurt
her by hurting myself like that?

We didn't think of our attempts
as a way to escape our grandmother
or our family.

We thought of our attempts
as a way for our family
to escape us.

We thought it was the most selfless gift we could give.
Jesus taught us selflessness.
Not Judas.

In Offense of *Commit* in Relation to Suicide on Trial

Exhibits A-H:

> It compares "truth" to "crime."
> It compares "patient" to "doctor."
> It compares "seeking release" to "seeking harm."
> It compares "contact protector" to "contact abuser."
> It compares "a chance to breathe" to "a chance to suffocate."
> It compares "seeking a form of heaven" to "seeking a form of hell."

Verdict:

> The defendant perpetuates making an insidious comparison between mental illness and prison.

Who judges the final language, the final lexicon, of the refusal to stay alive?

If You Stop Crying, It Won't Hurt As Much

It is another Monday night when my computer screen glows with my therapist giving me eye contact through her red rectangular glasses. Twenty-five year old me uncrosses their legs and faces her.

My therapist reminds me how I need to let her know what's coming up for me; to name my needs. The tears make my eyes fucking hurt. My chest feels lifted.

Alive

Before Taking Effexor for the First Time

prevent

suicidal thoughts/attempts

treat

living   interest in daily

restore   balance

Take

once daily

Swallow

the   trouble   whole

Paul's Response to His Jailer's Attempted Suicide

after Lindsay Young

"When the jailer woke up and saw the doors of the prison standing open, he drew his sword and was about to kill himself, because he assumed the prisoners had escaped." —Acts 16:27 NET

Hey. Look at me, man. I can't stop you from what you want to do or whatever thoughts emerge in your head. I *can* tell you that it is not your fault. You don't have to be trapped here anymore. Hey. Look at me, man. There is a light in these cavernous tunnels of ours. *Fuck* the end of it, because there's no *end* for us to get to. Hey. Look at me, man. How about we try living?

What Are You Watching Now?

Valencia: Rebecca, please. Promise me you'll never do it again.
Rebecca: I…I would love to promise you that. I'd love to promise you all that. But I can't.

—Gabrielle Ruiz (Valencia) and Rachel Bloom (Rebecca)
Crazy Ex-Girlfriend Season 3 Episode 6

I didn't see this soon enough on television.
The concept of healing overnight is a bandaid. Until this scene *landed* in my face!
As much as I love my family, I don't owe them pinky promises
when it comes to my mental health; honesty has to be much healthier than hope.

No one ever wants their loved one to die by suicide.
We make shooting star 11:11 birthday wishes and prayers for promises
of livelihood and happiness for them to face.
Through that effort, we don't talk enough about what makes us scared.

I didn't tell them how much I wanted to die even after my attempt of suicide.
Black people have the lowest rates of suicidal deaths, but we are still scared
of how to stay alive without the pressure. Scared because of the many deaths
we had before; including what isn't shown on television.

Sometimes the unexpected, remarkable gift
of television helps us see what's scary.
It's a form of hope
we need.

Consider this permission to not make promises.
Consider this permission to talk about suicide.
Consider this permission to crave this on television.

I Am *Living* for This!

Did you know children have suitcases now that can operate as scooters?!   Red and blue
zipping through DCA,   what a way to pass the time of a layover!   I am so in love
with that woman's braids.   What I'd give to feel fingers crafting   from my scalp to my
ends, to feel like a visual work of art.   A masterpiece.   The sweetness of the frosting of a strawberry donut…
Are   you   KIDDING   ME?!   So good.   I have two more pages of this book left,
and it's always   exciting   to start a whole new collection. My big purple backpack   fit   in the overhead bin
this time!   Hallelujah,   no forcing or stuffing today!   My partner and I watch the next episode
of *Feel Good*   and it is   stunning.   Neither of us are even aware   of the crying that's gonna come
four episodes later.   The closest thing to transformative justice on screen.   Justice has to come from
the internal too.   It is less humid in Portland.   Praise be!   Praise be to the gentle sun   and the on
time Lyft driver   with a clean vehicle.   Praise be   to the pink blossoms we witness   on the drive home.
Praise be to the warm shower   and Garnier Fructis conditioner.   Praise be to rest.   *Real* rest.
I am *living*   for all of this.   Praise be   to being *alive*   so I didn't miss it.

I Love It When Black People Ask, *How You Livin*?

More intentional than any *How are you doing?* I'll be asked in my lifetime.

How you livin'?

Just tryin' to be more like you.

The warmest hug from my friends and favorite cousins
I desire after not seeing them for so long.

How you livin'?

Ah, you know how it is.

The in-house check-in I can trust.

How you livin'?

Just hangin'.

The middle finger to suicide affecting our communities
and the slap in white supremacy's face for wanting us dead.

How you livin'?

You know you my homie, right?

The angel on my shoulder pushing me to be more open about my curses
in order to obtain more blessings.

How you livin'?

You know I love you, right?

The permission we call a prayer to live at all.

Acknowledgements

Thank you to the following publications that have published these poems, some under different titles or forms; some that are forthcoming—

Abbey of Hope's Reflectionary: "Jonah, Suicide, and GOD Doesn't Give You ANY More Than YOU CAN HANDLE"

A Gathering Together: "I Love it When Black People Ask, *How You Livin?*"

Amjambo Africa! : "Judas & Suicide"

Faith in Full Color: "Jonah, Suicide, and GOD Doesn't Give You ANY More Than YOU CAN HANDLE"

FreezeRay: "*What Are You Watching Now?*"

Maine Arts Journal: "In Defense of Commit in Relation to Suicide on Trial" and "In Offense of Commit in Relation to Suicide on Trial"

Misery Tourism: "Contracts"

Oxford University Press' Social Work and the Arts: Expanding Horizons: "Judas & Suicide," "In Defense of *Commit* in Relation to Suicide on Trial," "In Offense of Commit in Relation to Suicide on Trial," "I Hate to Go Inside a Building Created to Destroy Me," "The Devil is Concerned with More Pressing Matters Than My Mental Health Issues," and "Convince Us to Stay"

Pensive: a Global Journal of Spirituality and the Arts: "Paul's Response to His Jailer's Attempted Suicide" and "Side Effects of Prayer"

The Trill Project: "Convince Us to Stay"

University of New England School of Social Work Blog: "Before Taking Prozac for the First Time" and "Two Weeks After Taking Prozac for the First Time"

"A Facebook Message from My Stepmother" is an erasure of a Facebook message my stepmother sent me in 2018.

"Before Taking Effexor for the First Time" is an erasure of pharmaceutical instructions for VENLAFAXINE HCL ER 37.5 MG CAP.

"It Hurts a Lot More When the Reports Are Right" uses references from the *Substance Abuse and Mental Health Services Administration, Scientific American, American Journal of Nursing, and Mental Health America.*

"Judas & Suicide" along with some other poems in this book have been used for a Mad Horse Theatre Company production of the same name performed in April 2021.

"*Sick Boy*" is an erasure of the song "Sick Boy" by The Chainsmokers.

Gratitudes

Thank you to Game Over Books for giving the space and time this book needed before releasing it. Special thanks to Josh Savory, Catherine Weiss, and Sara Mae for believing in the manuscript and giving it a chance. I have loved this press for a long time. What a blessing to have y'all as a home for my first book.

Thank you to Eloisa Amezcua, Paige Lewis, R.A. Villanueva, Kaveh Akbar, Angel Nafis, Layli Long Soldier, Chet'la Sebree, Diana Khoi Nguyen, Christopher Gaumer, Gary Dop, Brittany Rogers, Ajanae Dawkins, Maurisa Li-A-Ping, Kelly Sue White, Aidan Daniel, Jeni Prater, Angela Dribben, LM Brimmer, Josh Nicolaisen, Kay Bancroft, Dana Krugle, Evan Mallon, and more at Randolph College for playing a huge role in my growth as a poet. Y'all are mesmerizing and amazing.

Thank you to Chrissy Margevicius, Daniel Garcia, and Robbie Dunning for first reading "Judas & Suicide" and providing feedback. Special thanks to Lynne Schmidt for not only providing feedback for "Judas & Suicide," but others in this collection in much earlier stages.

Thank you for residencies with Hewnoaks Artist Colony, Sundress Academy for the Arts (SAFTA), The Watering Hole, and the Words of Fire Retreat for the space to create a lot of these poems (especially the medication poems, the bible suicide poems, and the poems about the devil).

Thank you to the Quill Books & Beverage writing workshop on Sunday mornings and the Port Veritas open mic on Tuesday nights for hearing these poems in their drafted stages aloud. Thank y'all for the spaces to build poetry community in Maine. Thank y'all for your support.

Thank you to the lovely people at Quill Books & Beverage, Bull Feeney's, Third Place Portland, the Words of Fire Retreat, and the Weekly Email Chain Since April 2020 for the safe spaces to write and to all the beautiful people who are A LOT to name. I do hope you know who you are (and if you don't, I'll be sure to tell you to your beautiful face!).

Thank you to Art Amok Slam, Slam Free or Die, Beat Night, Cantab Lounge, and the Feminine Empowerment Movement Slam (FEMS) Tournament for the spaces to build poetry community outside of Maine and the spaces to read some of these poems aloud in their various stages of life.

Thank you to the committee at the Portland Public Library for selecting me as Portland, Maine's seventh poet laureate. Thank you to the community members who nominated me. Portland's community pushes me to be a better writer. Thank you.

Thank you to Word of Mouth (WOOOOOM! Comma, comma, ...bitch!) and to East Carolina University for being responsible for my career as a spoken word poet and a published poet.

Thank you to the University of New England for consistently celebrating my poetry and fellow poets' and artists' poetry.

Thank you to my best friend Mia S. Willis. Shout out to us not killing ourselves.

Thank you to Mia S. Willis and to the current and former Dying/Laughing team members Candace Frazier, Brenden Davis, and Shay Alexi for loving on my work and loving me. Let me continue to love on y'all's work and loving you. Follow Dying/Laughing on Twitter, Instagram, Facebook, and Patreon (where all episodes are FREE).

Thank you to MaineTransNet (follow on Twitter, Instagram, and Facebook under the same name) for supporting my art and poetry work on and off work hours. Trans people are extraordinary, and we are worthy of joy, thriving, and livelihood.

Thank you to organizations such as Maine Inside Out, Maine Youth Justice, Portland Outright, and Maine Prisoners Advocacy Coalition (follow all of them on Twitter, Instagram, and Facebook) for your incredible work and how you continue to teach me how to be of service to folks inside.

Thank you to my patrons on Patreon past and present: Adriana Gomez-Weston, Jan Bindas-Tinney, Jenn Carter, Michelle Brosseau, Tamara Ambrose, Hannah Allen, Stephanie Cotsirilos, Jocelyn Leighton, Rene' Goddess, Sam Fowler, Grant McPherson, Ahmad Kafari Muhammad, Jen Cragen, Julie Marie Hoey, Joanna NicciTina Free, Kimnada L. Bobb Jordan, Jake Fahey, Sampson Spadafore, Sneeetches, Allison Krzanowski, Stacey Koloski, Kate Hunter, Tarra Bouchard, Jeni Prater, Bridgette Kelly, Charlotte Bailey, and Liz Farmer.

Thank you to Dirigo Talent Agency for keeping me booked, and having clients go, "A poet and an actor?" Thank you to Mad Horse Theatre Company, PortFringe, Bare Portland, Speak About It, and Portland Stage for helping me find ways to integrate acting with poetry.

Thank you to Maine Humanities Council, Interfaith America, Network of Ensemble Theaters, The Portland Public Library, SPACE Gallery, The BTS Center, Quill Books & Beverage, Indigo Arts Alliance, Opera House Arts, The For Us, by Us Fund, Port Veritas, Creative Portland, Maine Writers & Publishers Alliance, The Apohadion Theater, Portland Museum of Art, Survivor Speak USA (deepest gratitude to Dee Clarke), The VIA Agency, Third Place Portland, Bendable, TEDxYouth at Cape Elizabeth High School, Black Table Arts, Equality Community Center, The Peace Studio, and Randolph College for supporting my work as a community artist, cultural worker, advocate, and poet. Thank you for the connections I have been able to make with fellow artists as well through your support.

Thank you to every Black poet I know (for those who fit this description as well as the descriptions throughout this list acknowledgments, yes, I'm thanking you twice as much).

Thank you Allison Raskin, Joshua Nguyen, Tanaya Winder, Lindsay Young, Chris Stedman, Paige Lewis, Indira Allegra, Danté Stewart, Katya Zinn, R.A. Villanueva, Raych Jackson, and Pádraig Ó Tuama for sitting with these poems and providing such generously loving blurbs.

Thank you to all five therapists I have had in my life. Special thanks to my current therapist since 2018 for playing the biggest and most recent role in my growth work.

Thank you to Mom, Byron, Dad, Miss Sylvia, Granny, Reece, Grandpa, Hawa, J.C., Danielle, Wayne, and the rest of my family who are A LOT to name. I do hope you know who you are (and if you don't, I'll be sure to tell you to your beautiful face!). Y'all always inspire me and support me to write. Please, never hesitate to ask me questions about my poems. I'm proud of us for continuing to grow and heal. Thank you for the reminder of how healing is nonlinear, and how healing is worthy of healthy boundaries, patience, love, and honesty.

Thank you to Johnathan Hinman. #redundant, I love you. Thank you for being there during my three initial rejections from Game Over Books as well as all the other rejections that have happened and will continue to happen. You're the best. Thank you to the whole Hinman family: Tom, Sandy, Jason, Sam, Jesse, and Alexis, as well; I'm always filled with gratitude for your support and love.

Thank you reader. I hope you and everyone else acknowledged are taking great precious care. I hope you and everyone else acknowledged are able to take needed breaks and breaths while reading. Each of your self care is more important to me than finishing this book in one sitting. You're under no obligation to read through an entire poem/set of poems that may make you feel unsafe. To the readers who may be uncomfortable more so because of learning something new, I encourage you to lean into that. Good job for accepting the awkwardness and discomfort in that regard.

Resources

If you or a loved one have been harmed by sexual violence, please refer to the following resources:

Rape, Abuse, & Incest National Network (RAINN) Hotline: 1-800-656-4673

The Network/La Red Hotline (for LGBTQ+ survivors): 1-800-832-1901 (toll free) /617-742-4911 (voice)

Stop It Now! (for child sexual abuse survivors): 1-888-773-2362

If you or a loved one is struggling with suicidality, please refer to the following resources:

National Suicide Prevention Lifeline: 988

Suicide Lifeline for Deaf or Hard of Hearing Folks: 711 then 988

Crisis Text Line: Text HOME to 741741

The Trevor Project (for LGBTQ+ youth): 1-888-628-9454 (or text START to 678678)

Transgender Lifeline: 1-877-565-8860

I know suicide prevention and awareness is far more systemic than what lifelines can provide, but I hope this is a step in knowing you're not alone. I'm so happy and filled with joy that many of you are still here. I want as many people here and alive as possible.

Biography

Maya Williams (ey/they/she) is a religious Black multiracial nonbinary suicide survivor who is the Poet Laureate of Portland, Maine from July 2021 to July 2024. *Judas & Suicide* is eir first full length collection. Maya was one of three artists of color selected to represent Maine in The Kennedy Center's *Arts Across America* series in 2020, and was listed as one of *The Advocate*'s Champions of Pride in 2022. Follow more of her work, and invite her to read or facilitate a workshop, at mayawilliamspoet.com.